DISCARDED
Bruce County Public Library
1243 MacKenzie Rd.
Port Elgin, Ontario  N0H 2C6

S0-BHR-241

SCHOLASTIC CANADA
BIOGRAPHY

# MEET
# Elsie MacGill

### ELIZABETH
### MACLEOD

### ILLUSTRATED BY
### MIKE DEAS

Scholastic Canada Ltd.
Toronto New York London Auckland Sydney
Mexico City New Delhi Hong Kong Buenos Aires

Elsie MacGill looked over the huge airplane factory. She knew she had to get these Hawker Hurricanes built as quickly as possible. There was a war on overseas. People were depending on her.

Elsie still had to perfect the plans and make sure the workers were assembling the planes correctly. It was a race against the clock.

What a huge challenge! But Elsie just got to work.

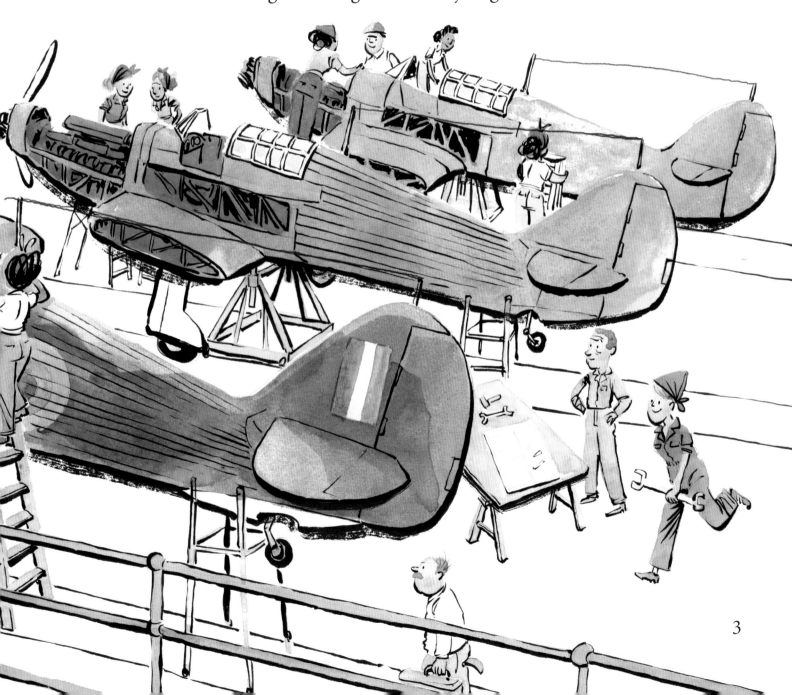

Elsie was born in Vancouver, British Columbia, in 1905. She had two older half-brothers, Eric and Frederic, and an older sister, Helen. Elsie and Helen were together so much the family called the pair HelNelsie.

One hundred years ago, many people thought girls shouldn't have as much schooling as boys. When Elsie was little, Canadian women were not even allowed to vote.

But Elsie's parents believed girls should get a good education. No wonder — Elsie's mother was one of the first women in Canada to become a judge.

Elsie's parents encouraged her to study hard. She even took drawing lessons from Emily Carr, who later became a famous painter.

Elsie was always repairing lamps, clocks and other gadgets for her family. Elsie loved figuring out how things worked, so she decided to study engineering.

Elsie impressed her professors and fellow students with how smart she was and how hard she worked. Thanks to her childhood art classes, she was especially good at drafting, or drawing, plans. But Elsie also liked to laugh and have fun. She made a lot of friends at school.

During the summers, "Miss Fix-It" worked in machine shops repairing motors. She learned more about many kinds of engines, hands-on.

In 1927, Elsie became the first woman in Canada to graduate with a degree in electrical engineering.

Later that year, Elsie began working for the Austin Company, an engineering firm in Pontiac, Michigan. She was a junior engineer and studied better ways to build cars.

Elsie worked hard but was often given unimportant tasks. She didn't enjoy her job very much.

8

The company was also involved in the airplane business. Elsie soon became fascinated by aeronautics, or how planes fly. So Elsie decided to study aeronautical engineering at the University of Michigan. She wanted to learn how to design and make airplanes.

Elsie passed all her courses for her master's degree in 1929. But the day before her graduation, something serious happened.

9

Elsie woke up with no feeling in her legs. She tried to move them — but couldn't!

Doctors told Elsie she had polio, a disease that can sometimes paralyze people or even kill them. Today we have a vaccine that protects against polio.

While still in hospital, Elsie was presented with her master's degree. She was the world's first woman with a graduate degree in aeronautical engineering.

It took Elsie three years to recover from her illness. She was eventually able to walk again using a cane.

Meanwhile, Elsie was determined to keep working. She wrote magazine articles about planes and continued to study them.

11

Soon after she recovered, Elsie's career really took off. She was offered a job at Fairchild Aircraft Limited in Longueuil, Quebec, in 1934.

At that time Canada was in the middle of the Great Depression, and many people were out of work. Elsie knew she was lucky to get a job — and this time doing real work on the planes she loved.

THIS WILL BE CANADA'S FIRST ALL-METAL PLANE. IT'S GOT TO BE RIGHT!

Elsie tested the company's airplanes in wind tunnels. She checked designs and did stress tests on the planes. She also worked on float planes, which can take off and land on water.

In 1938, Elsie got a new job in Thunder Bay, Ontario, at the Canadian Car and Foundry Company.

Elsie became its chief aeronautical engineer. She would be in charge of all airplane engineering work at the factory. Never before had a woman held such an important job working with planes.

One of Elsie's first projects was designing a plane known as the Maple Leaf Trainer II. She totally reworked the design of an older plane, making the wings stronger and changing the wheels and tail to make the plane more stable. Hers was the first plane designed by a woman.

Although Elsie had many projects to look after, the Maple Leaf Trainer II was soon ready for testing.

Most airplane designers let other people test their planes. Not Elsie! She couldn't fly them herself because her legs were too weak after her illness, but she rode along on the test flights.

That first test flight was especially dangerous. If any part of the plane failed, it could crash. But Elsie insisted flying was the best way for her to see how a new airplane was working.

Elsie loved her job designing planes. But the world was about to change.

In September 1939, Germany invaded Poland. That started World War II, the first war in which airplanes were really important.

Over the next few years, many other countries would become involved in the war. On one side was a group of countries that included Germany, Italy and Japan. On the other side were nations such as Britain, Canada, the Soviet Union and the United States.

By July of 1940, Germany had conquered most of Europe and wanted to invade Britain. To do that, it needed to destroy Britain's air force. So Germany started heavily bombing Britain and its airfields.

Britain needed more planes — lots of them. Britain especially wanted fighters called Hawker Hurricanes. And back in Canada, Elsie was ready to build them.

Using plans from Britain, Elsie built the machines and tools that would manufacture the Hurricane's 1500 different parts.

Elsie decided that each individual part would be identical for every plane. That way the pieces could be assembled quickly. Identical parts also meant planes could be repaired using parts from other planes. This would help the fighters get back in the air quickly, ready for battle again.

Thanks to Elsie, forty Hurricanes were delivered to England in the summer of 1940 — five months ahead of schedule.

To build all these planes, the factory's staff increased from 500 to 4500. About half of them were women. Many of the women had not worked in a factory before, so Elsie had to train them. It was tough, detailed work — assembling each plane took 800 steps. But Elsie inspired and respected her workers. She knew how to encourage them.

Between 1939 and 1943, Elsie's team built 1451 Hurricanes.

Hurricane fighters were also used in the Soviet Union during the war. This meant Elsie had to design a version of the plane that could fly in icy weather. She added skis so the plane could land on snow, and fitted de-icing systems on the propellers, tail and wings.

Back in the 1940s, it was very unusual for a woman to be in charge of such a technical project. Elsie became famous around the world.

In 1942, kids got to read about her incredible achievements when she starred in a comic called "Queen of the Hurricanes: Elsie MacGill."

In 1943, Elsie started her own company in Toronto helping airlines and companies that built airplanes with their designs.

Two years later, World War II ended. Canada's side had won, thanks in part to Elsie's Hurricanes.

In 1945, the United Nations (UN) organization was set up to help countries better work together.

A year later, Elsie became the first female technical advisor to the UN's International Civil Aviation Organization. Airplanes were becoming important for moving people, not only within Canada but around the world. Elsie helped make rules that made air travel safer for everyone.

In the 1960s, women's rights became Elsie's main focus. Elsie's career had flown high for decades. She'd always known there weren't many women in engineering, but Elsie had begun to see more clearly the obstacles that were holding them back. She encouraged women to get involved in politics in order to push for changes and make things fairer.

In 1967, the Royal Commission on the Status of Women in Canada was created. Elsie was named one of the commissioners. This important government group heard from people all over Canada about discrimination against women.

The Commission worked long hours. Sometimes people made fun of their work. It would have been easy to get discouraged, but Elsie never gave up.

In 1970, Elsie and the other members of the Commission gave Canada's federal government a list of ways to ensure equal opportunities for women. Many of their suggestions became law.

Elsie was already known all over the world for her pioneering work in aeronautics. Now she had become one of the most important people in Canada's women's movement. She received many awards and honours for both achievements.

Even after Elsie died in 1980, she continued to be given awards. She also had new ones named after her, including "The Elsie." The Elsie MacGill Awards are given out each year to recognize achievements of women in aviation.

Elsie blazed a trail for women in science and engineering. She also made Canada a better place for women, for girls and for everyone.

Elsie showed that the sky's the limit if you are determined and get down to work!

29

# Elsie MacGill's Life

| | |
|---|---|
| March 27, 1905 | Elizabeth "Elsie" Muriel Gregory MacGill is born in Vancouver, British Columbia. |
| 1927 | Elsie is the first woman in Canada to graduate with a degree in electrical engineering. |
| 1929 | Elsie contracts polio. |
| | Elsie receives her master's degree in aeronautical engineering from the University of Michigan, in the United States. That makes her the world's first woman to earn a master's degree in aeronautics. |
| 1934 | Elsie helps design the first all-metal aircraft built in Canada, the Super 71. |
| 1938 | Elsie becomes the first women to be a member of the Engineering Institute of Canada. |
| | Elsie designs the Maple Leaf Trainer II airplane for training pilots. |
| 1939–1945 | World War II. Canada builds 1451 Hawker Hurricanes for the Allied war effort. |

ELSIE AND HER BIG SISTER, HELEN.

ELSIE TOOK THIS PICTURE OF THE MAPLE LEAF TRAINER II. YOU CAN SEE HER SHADOW IN THE BOTTOM LEFT.

| | |
|---|---|
| 1946 | Elsie becomes the first woman technical advisor to the United Nations International Civil Aviation Organization. |
| 1953 | Elsie is named Woman Engineer of the Year by the American Society of Women Engineers. |
| 1967 | Elsie is appointed to the Royal Commission on the Status of Women in Canada. |
| 1975 | Elsie is awarded the Amelia Earhart Medal by the International Association of Women Airline Pilots. |
| Nov. 4, 1980 | Elsie dies in Cambridge, Massachusetts, United States. |
| 1983 | Elsie is made a member of Canada's Aviation Hall of Fame. |
| 1992 | Elsie becomes a member of the Canadian Science and Engineering Hall of Fame. |
| Nov. 15, 2017 | The Canadian government announces the Elsie Initiative for Women in Peace Operations. |

A PANEL FROM TRUE COMICS VOL. 1, NO. 8 JANUARY 1942, "QUEEN OF THE HURRICANES."

CANADA POST RELEASED THIS STAMP ON MARCH 27, 2019, ELSIE'S BIRTHDAY.

Dedicated to Sahara and Victoria Kyleman, future great Canadian women.
May you have Elsie MacGill's spirit of determination. Soar high!
Dedicated to you on behalf of your grandmother, Kathy.

— E.M.

For our future engineers and creators.

— M.D.

Many thanks yet again to amazing editor Erin O'Connor for piloting this book to completion.
Thanks also to Mike Deas for his great illustrations of Elsie and to the entire team at Scholastic.
I'm very grateful to Richard Bourgeois-Doyle, author and science administrator, and
Jim Van Dyk of the Canadian War Plane Museum for reviewing the manuscript and illustrations. Thanks as
well to my brothers John and Douglas. And special thanks to Paul for being my co-pilot!

— E.M.

**Scholastic Canada Ltd.**
604 King Street West, Toronto, Ontario M5V 1E1, Canada

**Scholastic Inc.**
557 Broadway, New York, NY 10012, USA

**Scholastic Australia Pty Limited**
PO Box 579, Gosford, NSW 2250, Australia

**Scholastic New Zealand Limited**
Private Bag 94407, Botany, Manukau 2163, New Zealand

**Scholastic Children's Books**
Euston House, 24 Eversholt Street, London NW1 1DB, UK

www.scholastic.ca

The illustrations were created using a blend of digital tools with traditional media.
Sketches were created with a Wacom tablet and Photoshop, then traced onto watercolour
paper, where colour and texture were added using gouache and watercolour paints.
Ink was used to add the black line to finish the art.

Photos ©: cover and title page speech bubble, top right: fatmayilmaz/iStockphoto;
Photos ©: 30 left: Courtesy of Elizabeth H. Schneewind and Helen Brock; 30 right: Canada Aviation and
Space Museum 16187; 31 left: Image courtesy Richard I. Bourgeois-Doyle; 31 right: Canada Post © 2019.

**Library and Archives Canada Cataloguing in Publication**

MacLeod, Elizabeth, author
Meet Elsie MacGill / Elizabeth MacLeod ; illustrated by Mike Deas.

(Scholastic Canada biography)
ISBN 978-1-4431-7020-8 (hardcover).--ISBN 978-1-4431-7021-5 (softcover)

1. MacGill, Elsie Gregory, 1905-1980--Juvenile literature. 2. Aeronautical
engineers--Canada--Biography--Juvenile literature. 3. Engineers--Canada--
Biography--Juvenile literature. 4. Women engineers--Canada--Biography--
Juvenile literature. 5. Feminists--Canada--Biography--Juvenile literature.
6. Social reformers--Canada--Biography--Juvenile literature. I. Deas, Mike,
1982-, illustrator II. Title.

TL540.M245M33 2019          j629.130092          C2018-905931-1

Text copyright © 2019 by Elizabeth MacLeod.
Illustrations copyright © 2019 by Mike Deas.
All rights reserved.
No part of this publication may be reproduced or stored in a retrieval
system, or transmitted in any form or by any means, electronic, mechanical,
recording, or otherwise, without written permission of the publisher, Scholastic
Canada Ltd., 604 King Street West, Toronto, Ontario M5V 1E1, Canada.
In the case of photocopying or other reprographic copying, a licence
must be obtained from Access Copyright (Canadian Copyright
Licensing Agency), www.accesscopyright.ca or 1-800-893-5777.

6 5 4 3 2 1          Printed in Malaysia 108          19 20 21 22 23

Bruce County Public Library
1243 MacKenzie Rd.
Port Elgin, Ontario N0H 2C6